SANTA MONICA
P U B L I C
L I B R A R Y

www.smpl.org

4-WEEK LOAN

TELEPHONE RENEWALS:
Main Library. 451-1866
Ocean Park Branch. 392-3804
Fairview Branch. 450-0443
Montana Branch. 829-7081

DATE DUE

NOV - 9 2002	
FEB 1 3 2003	
APR 2 2 2003	
MAY 1 0 2003	
FEB 1 4 2004	
JUN - 9 2005	

THE SECRET WORLD OF

Ants

THE SECRET WORLD OF

Ants

Theresa Greenaway

RAINTREE
Steck-Vaughn
PUBLISHERS

A Harcourt Company

Austin   New York
www.raintreesteckvaughn.com

Published by Raintree Steck-Vaughn Publishers, an imprint of Steck-Vaughn Company

Acknowledgments
Project Editors: Sean Dolan and Kathryn Walker
Illustrated by Stuart Lafford
Designed by Ian Winton

Planned and produced by Discovery Books

Library of Congress Cataloging-in-Publication Data

Greenaway, Theresa,
Ants / Theresa Greenaway.
p. cm. -- (Secret world of--)
Includes bibliographical references (p.).
ISBN 0-7398-3511-4
1. Ants--Juvenile literature. [1. Ants.] I. Title.

QL568.F7 G685 2001
595.79'6--dc21

00-062832

Printed and bound in the United States
1 2 3 4 5 6 7 8 9 0 LB 05 04 03 02 01

Contents

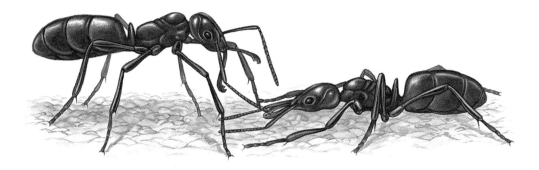

CHAPTER 1
Working as a Team

It has been estimated that there may be as many as 10,000 trillion ants alive at any time in the world!

The largest ant is the Bornean carpenter ant.

The smallest ants are tiny *Brachymyrmex* from South America and *Oligomyrmex* from Asia.

There are over 10,000 species, or kinds, of ants.

Ants are insects. They have six legs and a body divided into three parts. Together with crabs, spiders, centipedes, and other animals with a tough outer layer of cuticle and jointed legs, insects are arthropods. Ants are social insects, living in colonies that may contain many thousands of individuals.

Ants hatch from eggs into legless grubs. When full-grown, these turn into pupae. A pupa does not feed. Inside its tough outer case, the pupa changes into an adult ant. When this changeover, known as metamorphosis, is complete, the adult ant emerges. Unlike many other insects, most adult ants are wingless. Only young queen ants and male ants have wings.

An ant's body is made up of a head, a thorax, and an abdomen. An ant's head is equipped with eyes, a pair of long, jointed antennae or feelers, a pair of jaws, and a mouth. Behind the head is the thorax, which bears all six legs, and in the case of queen and male ants, two pairs of wings. At the other end of the ant's body is the abdomen. This is divided in two parts—a front part that is a narrow waist joined to the thorax, and a much larger rear part, called the gaster, that contains the gut and other organs. Most ants have venom glands in their abdomens, and some kinds also have stingers.

Most of the ants you see scurrying around are workers, like this ant. They can run fast on their six legs and are able to climb rough vertical surfaces, such as walls and tree trunks.

Abdomen
Some ants inject stinging venom from a stinger, others squirt it from the tip of the abdomen.

Thorax
This is the middle part of the body, to which all six legs are attached.

Jaws
These are sharp, so that the ant can bite enemies and snip up food.

Mouth
Liquids and food crushed by the jaws are eaten.

Antennae
An ant can smell and taste as well as feel with its very sensitive antennae.

WORLDWIDE ANTS

Ants live on all continents except Antarctica. There are ants in deserts, ants on high mountain slopes, ants in meadows, forests, and gardens. Ants often get into our houses, schools, and hospitals. Warmer countries have more kinds of ants than colder countries, but there is one kind of ant, *Leptothorax muscorum*, that even lives just inside the Arctic Circle.

THE COLONY

An individual ant cannot survive for very long on its own. It has to live with many others of its own kind in a colony. An ant colony is housed in a nest, where the young

Small, Medium, and Large

Some species of ants have several different kinds of workers. These form sub-castes of different sizes, called minor, medium, and major workers. Each sub-caste has its own job to do. Ants such as driver ants and leaf-cutter ants have large "major" workers with especially big sharp jaws that are called soldier ants. They guard the medium-sized foraging workers.

I DIDN'T KNOW THAT

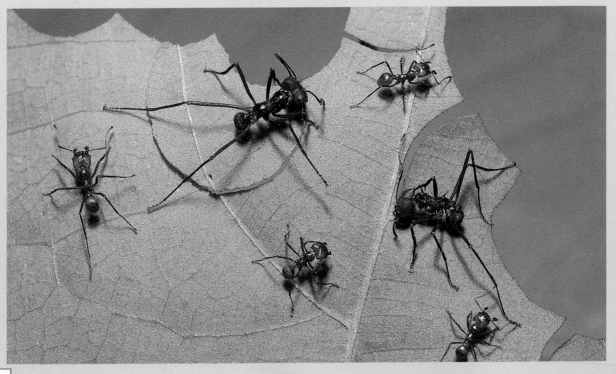

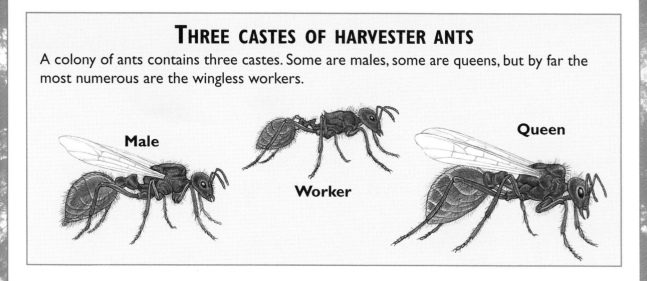

THREE CASTES OF HARVESTER ANTS

A colony of ants contains three castes. Some are males, some are queens, but by far the most numerous are the wingless workers.

Male

Worker

Queen

ants are reared and to which the ants return for shelter. Around the nest is an area, or territory, in which the ants search for food. The ants in a colony belong to groups called castes. Each caste has its own characteristic size. It also has its own role to play in the life and success of the colony.

CASTES

Most ants in a colony are workers. All workers are wingless, female ants. Although they are female, workers do not reproduce. As their name suggests, worker ants do all the work in the colony. They gather food, enlarge the nest, care for the eggs, larvae, and pupae, and look after and feed the queen ant, their mother. To carry out these tasks, workers often have much larger jaws than other

castes. Worker ants of species such as the black garden ant are all about the same size.

Each colony has at least one queen ant. The queen ant starts a new colony, but as soon as her first workers appear, she does no more work in the nest. A queen ant is larger than her workers and the male ants. She has a large abdomen because in a healthy, thriving colony, she lays all the eggs. Although ants such as harvester ants have colonies with only one queen, colonies of wood ants and others may have more than one queen.

Male ants are usually smaller than the queen ants. They do no work in the colony. Their only task is to fly away and mate with young queens, usually from another colony.

CHAPTER 2
Where Ants Live

We think of ants as living in the ground, but in fact, ants make their nests in many different places. Some spend almost their entire lives underground, seldom coming out into daylight. Many kinds of ants live in backyards, in gardens, and on farms, and are often seen running over paths or up and down walls. These ants, such as the black garden ants, nest near the surface of the ground. Others make nests above ground, in the treetops, or even inside some kinds of plants.

An ant's nest is a complex structure, with chambers at different levels. Ants use these chambers according to the time of day or the season of the year.

Leaf-cutter ants of Central and South American rain forests make nests over 300 feet (90 m) wide, reaching down to over 20 feet (6 m) underground.

African weaver ants live in treetops. A large nest has been known to extend across 17 treetops.

Tiny trapjaw ants live in small colonies inside split twigs.

A supercolony of Japanese wood ants covered an area of 675 acres (273 ha) on the island of Hokkaido.

LIFE IN AN ANT COLONY

Worker ants keep eggs clean and stop mold from growing on them.

Worker ants carry pupae from chamber to chamber in their jaws.

The queen ant lays all the eggs.

Wherever an ant colony is situated, an ant's nest is highly organized. Eggs, larvae, and pupae are kept in chambers connected by galleries so that the workers can run from one part of the nest to another. Some kinds of ants make special chambers where they dump their garbage. A lack of moisture is a serious threat to ant survival. Ants living in hot, dry places make tunnels deep into the ground to reach damper soil. They also build tunnels that allow air to enter or leave the nest—a kind of air conditioning. At night or in cold weather, some kinds of ants block the entrances of their nest with pieces of bark, small stones, or twigs.

Wood ant "anthills" are enormous. It is best to keep clear of them because hundreds of wood ants will rush to attack an intruder.

ANTHILLS

The wood ants of Europe and Asia often build their nests around a tree stump. They make a huge heap, or "anthill," of dry plant fragments, completely covering the stump. Underneath this, the ants dig chambers into the rotting wood and tunnels and more chambers into the ground below. In summer, it is warmest near the surface of the mound, so the ants tend the grubs and pupae there. In winter, the whole colony retreats into chambers deep underground, where there is no risk of frost.

HELPING TO MAKE SOIL

As ants make their nests in the ground, they are continually moving soil particles from place to place. Deeper layers are brought to the surface, and waste products from the ants help make the soil more fertile. In this way, ants play a part in soil formation. The harvester ants that live in the Painted Desert of Arizona move up to 1 ton of soil per acre (2.5 metric tons per ha) during their nest-making activities.

LIVING INSIDE A THORN

The bull's horn acacia tree grows in Central America, and it has a special partnership with certain species of ants. Like all plants, its fresh green leaves attract caterpillars, aphids, and other insects that feed on them. Fierce Aztec ants make their nests inside its large thorns. These ants kill any insect that lands on the acacia and feed the insect to their grubs. They also snip off climbing plants that try to grow over the acacia and keep the ground beneath it free from seedlings. In return, the tree produces fatty lumps at the tips of its leaves that the ants enjoy eating.

WEAVING A NEST

Weaver ants make nests inside a cavity formed by the large leaves of tropical trees. Ants first pull up the edge of a leaf. Then they summon more and more workers, who grip the edges of the leaf. Other workers grip these workers on the legs or waist, so that a chain of workers is made. The last of the chain holds onto the edge of another leaf. When two leaves have been pulled toward each other, another worker picks up a larva that is almost ready to pupate. When the

Like the Aztec ant, the acacia ant also lives in the thorns and stems of acacia trees. At the tip of most acacia leaflets there is a fatty lump that the ants eat.

grub is squeezed, it produces a drop of silk. The worker carries the grub to and fro, joining the leaves with silk "stitches."

Weaver ant workers have powerful jaws that act like pincers, holding tightly to the edges of the leaves that make the walls of their nest.

I DIDN'T KNOW THAT

Chewed to a Pulp

Carpenter ants are large ants that chew wood and other plant material into a pulp that is used to make the walls of their nest. In tropical forests, the ants use fallen branches as the raw material for their nests. When these ants live close to human villages, they can cause a lot of damage to buildings by chewing through wooden walls, decking, and wooden support structures.

CHAPTER 3
Senses

For the ant colony to operate in a coordinated way, the hundreds or thousands of ants it contains must be able to communicate with each other. They have to work together to build the nest and all its underground chambers, tunnels, air passageways, and entrance holes.

Ants also need to recognize a threat and quickly summon enough fellow workers to drive away or kill the enemy. Any ant-eating predator that manages to break into the nest and eat the young ants, and maybe even the queen herself, may cause the end of the entire colony.

These wood ants are members of the same colony. They are communicating an unknown message to each other.

Each species of ant is thought by biologists to have a vocabulary of between 10 and 20 chemical "words."

Like dogs and foxes, weaver ants use their droppings to mark their territory. This warns weaver ants from other nests to stay away.

Wood ants can detect movements at a distance of about 4 inches (10 cm).

An alarmed leaf-cutter ant makes a sound by rubbing a tiny ridged area of the abdomen against part of its waist to warn other workers of a threat.

Citronella ants make a substance that smells strongly of lemons from glands in their heads. This alerts other ants to danger and helps to scare off enemies.

Worker ants also have to find food, and male and queen ants have to be able to recognize each other.

Of course, ants cannot sit down and discuss things the way people do, but their way of communicating with each other is quite remarkable. Ants have senses of sight, smell, hearing, and touch, and they can "talk" to each other using chemicals. Ants release a variety of different substances from glands in different parts of their bodies, including their heads and their abdomens. Other workers can detect and identify these, so that they know whether their nestmate is warning of danger or telling them about a new food source.

These weaver ant workers are working together to carry a dead bug back to the other members of the colony.

SIGHT

Like many other insects, ants have one pair of compound eyes. Each of these is made up of hundreds of tiny units, each with its own lens. Compound eyes are very good at detecting movement, but most ants do not have particularly good eyesight.

TWO QUEENS

If there is more than one queen ant in a nest, one queen challenges the other. She stands tall and threatens the other queen with open jaws. To avoid being bitten and killed, the second queen communicates submission by lying very flat against the ground.

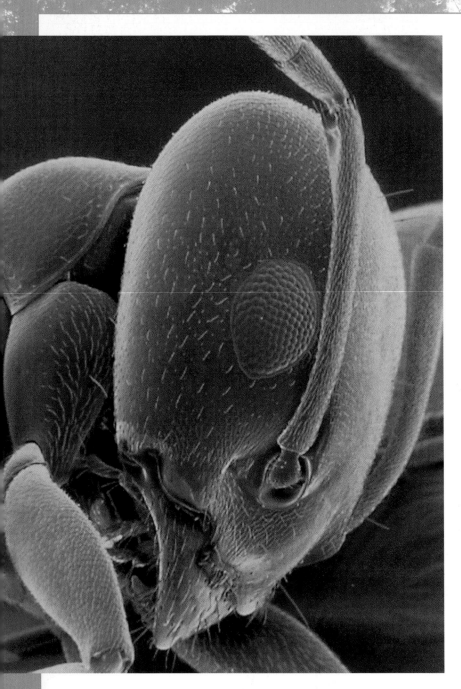

This ant's compound eye has been colored blue in this highly magnified (stereoscan) photograph.

each other with their antennae. An ant that wants to be fed by a returning worker taps it on part of the mouth. This stimulates the well-fed ant to regurgitate, or vomit, droplets of food.

CHEMICAL CONVERSATIONS

Without doubt, an ant's sense of smell is of great importance. Ants use the smelly chemicals they produce in combinations that have many different meanings. Chemicals that are used to lay trails are produced in glands at the rear of the ant. Some of these show the way to a new source of food. Others indicate that the trail-layer has found a good site for a new part of the nest. Another is used in trails indicating an enemy a long way away from the nest.

SENSITIVE FEELERS

On its head, just behind its mouth, each ant has a pair of jointed antennae, or feelers. These antennae are highly sensitive to touch, smells and even vibrations. When two ants from the same nest meet, they touch

Queen Odors

Ants from the same nest can recognize each other by their smell. This smell is a mixture of smells from three sources. The most important of these comes from the queen. The queen's scent is spread all around the colony by the workers tending to her. The second comes from the workers. Because they are all in such close contact, odors from the workers, who are all sisters, are spread from one to another. The third part of the colony's smell comes from the nest itself.

Alarm chemicals that alert nest-mates to an enemy close by are produced in glands in the ant's head. They work to alert other workers to help the first ant overcome the enemy. These chemicals vaporize, or change to a gas, in the air, and are picked up by the antennae. One chemical sounds the alarm. The next tells the ants to run to the site of danger. Other chemicals stimulate the alerted workers to attack and bite the enemy.

CHAPTER 4
Food and Feeding

Ants cut food into pieces small enough to chew and swallow with a pair of jaws, or mandibles. These can open wide or close tightly together. Different species of ants have jaws that are suited to dealing with different kinds of food. Most ants are predators that catch and eat other insects and invertebrates. By working as a team, they can overcome animals, such as centipedes, that are much larger than a single ant. A large nest of foraging ants helps to keep the populations of many kinds of insects in check. Some of these, such as leaf-eating caterpillars, are pests of farm crops and garden plants.

These driver ants are killing an assassin bug, which is itself a fierce predator of other insects.

A colony of wood ants can gather over 100,000 caterpillars in just one day.

The long pincer-like jaws of trap-jaw ants can snap shut in less than one-thousandth of a second.

A *Thaumatomyrmex* ant has mandibles with very long, thin teeth. It uses these to pick up and carry its prey, a very bristly kind of millipede.

Campanotus detritus lives in the Namib Desert, where it gets moisture when sea fogs condense on the sand.

Ants soon take advantage of a new food source. They will even enter houses to eat left-over pet food.

Ants also need water. In most parts of the world, water is easy to find, but in hot, dry areas, ants may have to travel some distance to find it. Workers of a large hunting ant that lives in tropical America carry droplets of water back to

Droplets of dew are often the only source of water for ants that live in the Namib Desert of western Africa.

their nest between their jaws. Any water that is not needed by ants in the nest is used to moisten the walls of the nest.

SPREADING THE NEWS

If an ant that is out foraging finds a good supply of food, it eats what it can, then returns to its nest. To allow itself and other workers to find the new food again, it lays a scent trail from the food back to the nest.

FEEDING NESTMATES

Worker ants tending the nest and larvae, and the larvae themselves, have to be fed by the foraging workers. The hungry worker usually taps or strokes a worker that has returned to the nest until it is given food. The returning worker gives food by vomiting some of what it has eaten.

HONEYPOTS

In honeypot ant colonies, special workers called "repletes" hang from the roof of their nest and are fed nectar by other workers returning from foraging trips. Eventually, they are so full that

Ants will share their food with hungry nestmates, but only if the hungry ant makes the correct signal that it needs food.

The abdomen of each "replete" is enormously swollen with nectar fed to them by foraging workers.

their abdomens are just swollen sacs. When food is short, the colony can survive on its own food supply. The bulging repletes regurgitate droplets of sugary liquid for the other workers to eat.

LEAF-CUTTING ANTS

All day, worker leaf-cutter, or parasol, ants climb bushes and trees, snipping out pieces of leaves and flower petals that they carry back to their nest.

Here, the leaf fragments are passed to other, smaller workers called gardeners. The gardeners use the pieces of leaf to grow a special kind of fungus in underground chambers. The ants and the ant grubs all feed on the fungus.

Because leaf-cutter ants sometimes carry pieces of leaf high above their heads, they are called "parasol" ants.

21

Ant Cows

Soft-bodied aphids, which are sap-sucking insects, drink sugary sap in order to obtain enough protein to grow. As a result, they produce droplets of concentrated sugary liquid called honeydew as waste. Ants such as the black garden ant and wood ant love this liquid so much that they tend clusters of aphids and stroke them to release more liquid. The ants also protect these aphids from aphid predators.

When it first hatches, the caterpillar of the large blue butterfly feeds on wild thyme. Then it crawls over the ground until it is found by ants that carry it into their nest.

CURIOUS PARTNERSHIPS

Some butterfly caterpillars have a strange partnership with ants. In Europe, the large blue and the rebeli butterflies have caterpillars that feed on flowers for the first few weeks after they hatch. Then they drop to the ground, where they are found by certain species of foraging ants.

These ants carry the larvae back to their nest. Here, the large blue caterpillar actually feeds on the ant larva, but the rebeli caterpillar is fed by the worker ants as if it were an ant grub. In return, these caterpillars ooze out a sweet substance that the ants find very tasty.

SEED GATHERERS

In many dry parts of the world, including deserts, harvester ants collect seeds. They store them in nest chambers called granaries. Special workers with short but broad, powerful jaws crack open the seeds, and the softer parts inside are then fed to the grubs. Some of the seeds gathered by these ants are left uneaten. Buried in the fertile soil of the ants' nest, they can start to grow. So as well as eating seeds, ants also help to disperse, or spread, seeds away from the parent plant.

If this seed is not eaten by ant grubs in the harvester ant's nest, then it may germinate and grow.

CHAPTER 5
Reproduction

When the time is right for ants to reproduce, the young winged queens and the winged males crawl out of their nests and fly into the air. Males and females from the same nest are usually brothers and sisters. So that they mate with unrelated ants, all the nests of the same kind of ant in an area seem to swarm at once. Suddenly the sky is full of flying ants. This means that there is a good chance that males and females from different nests will meet up and mate.

After mating, male ants flutter to the ground and die. The young queen ants also return to the

As winged males and young queens leave the nest, many workers also swarm out to protect them.

A queen ant mates just once. She stores enough male sex cells in a sac in her abdomen to last for the rest of her life.

A queen leaf-cutter ant lays one egg every two seconds for up to ten years. During this time, she produces up to 150 million daughter worker ants.

Most queen ants do not survive long enough to start a colony. They are eaten by predators.

Unmated driver ant queens do not have wings. They have to wait for winged males to fly to them.

ground, where they bite off their mate's wings or snap them off with their legs. The mated queen immediately looks for a suitable place to begin a new colony. She makes a small nest and starts to lay the eggs. While the first adult worker ants are developing, she has no help and so must look after these

If more than one male attempts to mate with the same queen ant, they all fall to the ground, where the males continue their struggle.

first eggs and grubs herself. During this time, she does not eat. Instead, her now useless wing muscles are broken down to give her the food she needs to start her new colony.

FLYING FRENZY

Ants often choose a warm, humid day in summer to mate. As winged males and females leave their nest for the first and last time, hundreds of workers run around them. In the eastern United States, one of the most common ants is known as the Labor Day ant because this species always swarms around that date. People cannot fail to notice as hundreds of winged ants swarm out of cracks in sidewalks and lawns and take off to mate on the wing. Many of these mating pairs are eaten by flying birds and insects such as dragonflies. Many others are squashed by cars or people's feet when they land on

It's hard not to notice flying ants when they swarm out of their nests and take to the air by the thousands.

roads or sidewalks, or drown if they land on water. Only a very few of the hundreds of queen ants that left a nest are successful in starting their own colony.

HARD-WORKING WORKERS

A queen ant lays hundreds, thousands, or millions of eggs in her lifetime. Each tiny egg is

For their size, ants can lift amazingly heavy objects. This ant is carrying a really large grub in its jaws.

tended by worker ants, who keep it clean and make sure that it is kept at the right temperature. They move the eggs closer to the surface for warmth, or to deeper chambers of the nest if it is too hot and dry. The eggs hatch into tiny grubs, or larvae. Ant grubs cannot look after themselves. Worker ants feed, clean, and look after them.

MOLTING

Ant grubs, just like adult ants, are covered with a tough outer cuticle. This does not stretch, so in order to grow, each grub has to molt. During molting, the cuticle splits, and the grub wriggles out. Until the new skin hardens, it is stretchy. An ant grub molts three times, then it is ready to pupate.

EGG TO ANT

As the eggs are laid by the queen (1), they are tended by worker ants until they hatch into grubs. These grubs are then fed and kept clean by the workers (2). When they are ready to pupate, some grubs spin cocoons around themselves (3). The young ants are pale and soft when they first emerge from their cocoons (4) but soon become darker and harden.

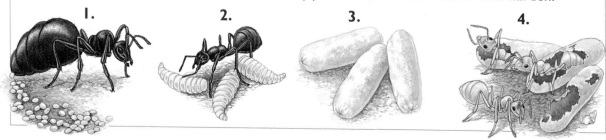

1.   2.   3.   4.

PUPATION

Ants with only one waist segment, such as wood ants, have grubs that spin a silk cocoon around themselves. Inside, the grub changes into an adult ant. Ants that have two waist segments, such as bulldog ants, do not have grubs that spin cocoons. The pupa looks like a pale but immobile adult, with its legs tucked close to its sides. When the change from grub to adult is complete, the outer skin of the pupa splits, and a new ant wriggles out. The adult ant is full-grown, and does not molt again.

All fertilized eggs develop into female ants, either workers or queens. Only unfertilized eggs develop into male ants.

MALES OR FEMALES?

A queen ant is remarkable. She decides which sex her eggs will be. At first, she needs plenty of workers, so she produces eggs that she fertilizes with the male sex cells that she has stored in her abdomen. These develop into female worker ants. As her colony grows, some of these female grubs are given extra food and are kept warmer than the others. These develop into new queen ants. The queen then lays some unfertilized eggs. These develop into male ants.

WHEN THE QUEEN DIES

Most colonies have just one queen. She is the mother of all the ants in the colony. A queen may live for many years, but eventually she grows old and dies. What happens then? Some of the workers may be able to lay a few eggs, but because these ants have never mated, the grubs that hatch from them are all males. Gradually, the workers die. The colony is doomed.

Pharoah's Ant

This tiny ant originally lived only in the tropics but has now spread to many other parts of the world. It builds nests in heating ducts and hollow walls of houses, enjoying the warmth from the central heating. It is quite a pest! Queen Pharoah's ants have unusually short lives, just three months, but the young queens mate with males from their own colony. Each starts a new nest at the edge of the main colony, eventually producing a huge supercolony.

I DIDN'T KNOW THAT

CHAPTER 6
A Fearsome Army

Army ants from tropical South and Central America and driver ants from Africa have a fearsome reputation for eating everything in their path—even human babies. Is this true? Actually, army ant raids travel too slowly to catch animals such as lizards, small mammals, or people. However, a swarm of driver ants spreads out into a huge fan which is hard to avoid. Their victims are known to include a python that had just swallowed its prey and was unable to move quickly, a tethered donkey, and a gorilla. Even an unwatched human baby has been killed by voracious driver ants.

When army ants are on the move, every living thing in their path struggles to get out of the way.

A raiding party of army ants contains up to 200,000 ants and may be 66 feet (20 m) wide.

The encroaching army ants move forward at about 46 feet (14 m) an hour.

African driver ants have the largest colonies of any insect—just one may contain over 16 million insects.

Driver ants strike fear in the hearts of humans because they have large, sharp jaws. Being bitten by hundreds of them at a time is a painful experience.

People leave their houses when army or driver ants pass through. They know that the ants will clear their houses of cockroaches and other pests.

Soldier army ants have extremely large, powerful jaws. Their job is to protect the foraging workers.

Most of the animals killed and eaten by these invading hordes are other insects, including other species of ants, spiders, and other invertebrates. After a swarm has been through, the forest floor or grassland is cleared of almost all its ant and invertebrate life. The next time the army or driver ant colony goes out on a raid, it chooses a different direction. This ensures that the ants get enough to eat and that each raided area has enough time to recover before it is raided again.

ARMY ANTS

In the rain forests of South and Central America, colonies of army ants have a cycle of activity that lasts 35 days. This cycle is divided into two phases. In the statary phase, all ant grubs in the colony pupate, and after 10 days, the queen lays thousands of new eggs. During this phase, the colony stays in the same site, but raiding parties go out to bring back food for the ants tending the queen, eggs, and pupae. The new workers emerge from their pupae at the same time that the eggs hatch into larvae. The whole colony then enters a second phase, called the nomadic phase. The entire colony travels through the rain forest, making a new nest, called a bivouac, every night.

Camp Followers

Many other kinds of animals follow the raids of army ants. The bicolored antbird and the antwren (below) feed on insects that fly up to escape from the marching ants. Some species of rain forest butterflies follow behind to feed on antbird droppings. Other insect-eating predators stay nearby to catch any insects that manage to escape from the ants.

Bivouacs are made on the side of a tree trunk or large limb. The bivouac is made by hundreds of workers clinging to each other's bodies. They make a kind of ant-basket that contains the queen, the larvae, and the workers tending them. If they cluster tightly together, the temperature inside the bivouac increases. If they loosen up, it cools.

RAIDING PARTIES

In the statary phase, raiding parties of army ants never cover the same ground twice. They travel in a slightly different direction every day. By hunting in such large parties, army ants are able to overcome entire nests of other ant species, as well as crickets, spiders, and centipedes.

DRIVER ANTS

In Africa, driver ants also go out on raids. Unlike army ants, driver ants have underground nests. These nests are large,

with a spreading network of tunnels and chambers hidden beneath the surface of the soil. Workers swarm out of the nest in a column that spreads out into smaller lines of ants, like the branches and twigs of a tree. At the front edge of the swarm, the ants kill everything too slow to escape. Ants snip off morsels of their victims and carry them back to the

Soldier driver ants are much larger than the workers that they guard.

nest. All the flesh is stripped off a small mammal, leaving only the bones. As some workers leave the front line, they are replaced by others coming up from behind. After a few hours on the rampage, the ants turn around and swarm back into the nest.

CHAPTER 7
Ant Warfare

Ants are extremely aggressive. At the slightest threat to their nest, they spring to the attack. An ant attacks in one of two ways. It opens its jaws wide and bites, holding on to its enemy no matter how large. Then it swings its abdomen forward. Ants such as wood ants then spray a stinging, burning liquid from a venom gland into the wound made by the jaws. Bulldog ants, fire ants, and others actually have stingers that they use to inject their venom. Although the effect of just one ant may be quite easy to ignore, the combined attacks of tens or even hundreds is not.

These two fighting ants are the same species but are from different nests. The loser will be killed and eaten.

Colobopsis ants have special large-headed workers that block the entrance to their nests so that other kinds of aggressive ants cannot get in.

Workers of a Malaysian ant, *Campanotus saundersi*, have large glands that contain poisonous liquids. When these ants are attacked, they burst, covering their enemy with poison and committing suicide in the process.

Honeypot ant workers stand on top of pebbles with their legs stretched out like stilts, in order to seem larger than they really are.

Fire ants get their name because it feels as if your skin is on fire when these fierce little ants sting.

This desert ant is about to indulge in chemical warfare. It has bent its abdomen forward to spray stinging, toxic venom over its enemy.

Ants attack other ants—those of different species and even other colonies of the same species. Why do they do this? The main reason is that a colony of ants needs a large amount of food if it is to thrive and grow. For most ants that have a permanent nest site, there is a limit to how far foraging workers can travel every day in their search for food. So it is important for them that all the available food should be theirs alone. They do not want to share it with other ants.

SMALL IS RISKY

A small ant colony is always at risk of attack from a larger colony of the same species. Workers seem to know whether a neighboring colony is smaller or larger than their own. If they decide it is smaller, an all-out attack is launched. Ants kill each other by biting off antennae, legs, or snipping each other in half at the waist. Those that sting do so in ant-to-ant conflict. Victorious ants carry the corpses of their victims back to feed their own grubs. They may even raid the vanquished colony, taking pupae and grubs back to work for them.

Sometimes small groups of newly mated queens start a colony together. The advantages are that the colony grows more quickly than if just one queen sets up a home by herself. As these colonies with many queens grow, the queens engage in a power struggle that results in the death of all except one. Dominant queens threaten more submissive ones, and the workers often attack and kill the losers.

Killer Ants

The bites and venoms of most kinds of ants cause pain to people who are attacked but are rarely serious. The Australian bulldog ant is an exception. It has a venom strong enough to kill humans who are allergic to it. Thirty stings may be fatal, and if you accidentally disturb a bulldog ant's nest, a lot more than 30 angry ants may attack you.

I DIDN'T KNOW THAT

HOUSE ARREST

Tiny *Forelius pruinosus* ants from Arizona steal food from honeypot ant workers, and they can also prevent the larger honeypot ants from foraging for food, even around their own nest site. Large numbers of the smaller ants cluster around the entrances of the honeypot ants' nest. As honeypot ant workers try to leave their nest, they are driven back by a chemical spray. Another related ant, *Conomyra*, drops a hail of tiny stones down the entrance holes, as well as spraying foul-smelling chemicals.

Raiding Amazon ants seize wood ant pupae in their jaws and carry them away. When these stolen workers emerge, they look after the Amazon ants and their nest.

SLAVE-MAKING ANTS

Amazon ant workers are fierce fighters but cannot make nests or look after themselves at all. Instead, they raid wood ant nests, killing the workers and stealing the pupae, which they carry back home to work as slaves. When the wood ant workers emerge from these stolen pupae, they look after the Amazon ants, caring for their eggs and grubs and feeding the workers.

CHAPTER 8
Enemies of Ants

Left alone, most ants do little or no harm to people. Some kinds are so rare that they are seldom seen. Ants can be beneficial, eating pests and improving the soil, but they can also be harmful, and many have painful bites and stings.

Ants become pests when they undermine the roots of crops and garden plants by building their nest among them. Leaf-cutter ants are a serious nuisance on a

Fruit trees are sprayed to kill insect pests, but the sprays will also kill the ants that eat some of those pests.

Basiceros ants, which live in the American tropics, hide themselves from ant-eating enemies by covering themselves with fine particles of soil that get stuck on their hairy bodies.

Harvester ant workers keep spiders from catching them in webs by closing nearby nest entrances and staying inside.

A termite-eating ant from the southwestern United States goes out hunting only at a time of day when parasitic flies that would attack it are not active.

An aardvark can close its nostrils to prevent ants from crawling inside.

The Brazilian fire ant has been accidentally imported into the United States. They are now a painful nuisance in Texas.

tropical fruit plantation, where they strip trees of foliage. Occasionally ants enter houses and infest food stores or even chew away structural timbers. When ants do become pests, humans try to get rid of them, sometimes by using chemical pesticides.

Ants also have many natural enemies, or predators, that eat ants. Although one ant is not much of a meal, a whole nest of

Leaf-cutter ants have stripped many of the leaves on this tree down to the ribs. This can be serious damage on a plantation of tropical fruit trees.

ants, plus eggs, grubs, and pupae, can add up to quite a feast. Even some quite large mammals break into ants' nests, and gobble up as many as possible. Birds, lizards, and other insects such as beetles also prey on ants, but for many ants, their worst enemies are other ants.

ANT-EATING MAMMALS

For the animals that eat them, it is vital that as many ants as possible are caught and swallowed before they scurry away underground, taking grubs and pupae with them. Mammals whose diet consists mostly of ants and termites can do just this. Termites are not related to ants, but like ants they are insects that live in enormous colonies.

Animals that specialize in eating ants include the short-beaked echidna from Australia, the giant

Armadillos eat ants as well as other insects and soft fruit. Scientists in Texas discovered that one armadillo had eaten **40,000** ants in one meal!

anteater, tamandua, and silky anteaters from South America, and the aardvark, which lives in Africa. Echidnas and anteaters are all toothless, but they have very long, sticky tongues so they can pick up lots of ants extremely quickly. The giant anteater, tamandua, and silky anteater also have long powerful claws to rip open ants' nests.

PARASITIC FLIES

A parasite is an animal that feeds on or in another living animal. As they snip up and carry home pieces of leaf, medium-sized leaf-cutter ant workers are at risk from parasitic flies. These flies need to lay eggs on the ants so that each of their own grubs can feed and develop inside a worker ant. To prevent this, tiny leaf-cutter workers, called minims, ride on the pieces of leaf and attack any parasitic fly that comes too near.

The extraordinarily long sticky tongue of the silky anteater is ideal for catching ants as they try to escape from the tree nest that the anteater has just ripped open.

ANT-EATING BIRDS

Birds that peck up ants seem able to ignore the bites and stings of their enraged victims. In the United States, the common flicker is a woodpecker that spends much of its time on the ground eating ants. In Europe, the green woodpecker does the same, even stabbing its beak into large wood ant mounds!

When flying male and female ants take off on their mating flight, ant-eating birds, such as swifts and fly-catchers, are ready and waiting to catch them in the air. On the ground, pheasants, hens, and partridges are among the many other kinds of birds that peck up the newly mated queens as they return to earth and shed their wings.

UNINVITED GUESTS

The moth-butterfly caterpillar of Australia catches and eats weaver ant grubs, and the workers are powerless to prevent it. The caterpillar has a leathery, shieldlike back. It clings very tightly to the leafy wall of the weaver ant's nest. When it is hungry, it raises itself slightly and engulfs a number of ant grubs. Then it clamps down hard and eats them. Ants cannot bite through or wriggle under this tough shield.

Like most woodpeckers, the green woodpecker eats many kinds of insects, but this species is particularly fond of ants. It strikes an ant's nest on the ground with its beak and picks up the ants with its long, sticky tongue.

Tasty!

In some parts of the world, people eat ants! Weaver ants are eaten in some parts of the Philippines, and honeypot ants are dug up by Australian aborigines. The sugary liquid that each replete contains is very similar to honey. Different kinds of honeypot ants are collected and eaten by rural people in Mexico.

THE FUTURE OF ANTS

Ants and their capacity for social organization are among the most fascinating aspects of the natural world. A lot is now known about the lives of many different kinds of ants, but there is still much more to be discovered about the rest. It is important to conserve the habitats in which they live, especially those of the rarest and most specialized kinds.

This ant is in an alert posture in its rain forest home in Trinidad. People also have to stay alert—to make sure that rain forests all around the world are conserved for ants and other wildlife.

43

Glossary

ABDOMEN – The back part of an ant's body, consisting of a narrow waist and a gaster

ANTENNAE – A pair of jointed "feelers" on the head of the ant, which are highly sensitive to touch, smell, and vibration

ARTHROPODS – Invertebrate animals that have a tough outer layer called a cuticle, or exoskeleton, and jointed legs

COCOON – The silk case that some kinds of ant larva spin around themselves before pupating

COLONY – A large number of animals of the same species, living closely together

COMPOUND EYE – An eye made up of hundreds of tiny units, each with its own lens

CUTICLE – The tough outer layer, or exoskeleton, of an arthropod that supports and protects the body within it

GASTER – The rear part of the ant's abdomen that contains the gut and other organs

GLAND – An organ in an animal's body that produces specific substances

GRUB – The wormlike larva stage of an ant's life cycle after it has hatched

INVERTEBRATES – Animals that do not have a backbone

LARVA (plural: larvae) – A stage in the life cycle of an animal that hatches from an egg but has not yet attained adult form

MANDIBLES – A pair of jaws

METAMORPHOSIS – The changeover from pupa to adult ant

MOLT – To shed the entire outer layer of skin

PARASITE – An animal that feeds on or in another animal

PREDATOR – An animal that hunts another animal for food

PREY – An animal that is caught and eaten by another animal

PUPA (plural: pupae) – The stage in the life cycle of an ant when it changes from a larva into an adult

QUEEN ANT – A female ant that mates with a male and then lays all the eggs in an ant colony

SOLDIER ANTS – Worker ants that are larger than the other workers, and whose job it is to defend the ant colony

SWARM – The movement of a colony or large group of ants

THORAX – The middle part of an ant's body to which the legs are attached

WORKER ANT – A wingless female ant that does not reproduce but looks after the young ants, collects food, and keeps the nest clean

Further Reading

Colombo, Luann. *The Ant Book and See-Through Model*. Kansas City, MO: 1994.

Fowler, Allan. *Inside an Ant Colony*. Danbury, CT: Children's Press. 1998.

Hartley, Karen and Marco, Chris. *Ant*. Chicago: Heinemann, 1998.

Robinson, W. Wright. *How Insect Build Their Amazing Homes*. Woodbridge, CT: Blackbirch, 1999.

Sabine, Francene. *Amazing World of Ants*. Mahwah, NJ: Troll, 1997.

Web sites

Mymrecology: The Scientific Study of Ants

www.mymrecology.org

Information and scientific facts about ants. Contains material about classification, colony founding, nest building, and foraging strategies. Also offers tips and guidelines for building artificial nests and starting ant colonies at home.

Acknowledgments
Front cover: Eric Soder/Natural History Photographic Agency; p.8: K.G.Preston-Mafham/Premaphotos; p.11: William S.Paton/Bruce Coleman Collection; p.12: K.G.Preston-Mafham/Premaphotos; p.13 top: Kim Taylor/Bruce Coleman Collection; p.13 bottom: Frank Schneidermeyer/Oxford Scientific Films; p.14: Stephen Dalton/Natural History Photographic Agency; p.15: K.G.Preston-Mafham/Premaphotos; p.16: Tina Carvalho/Oxford Scientific Films; p.17: J.A.L.Cooke/Oxford Scientific Films; p.18: K.G.Preston-Mafham/Premaphotos; p.19: Anthony Bannister/Natural History Photographic Agency; p.20: Satoshi Kuribayashi/Oxford Scientific Films; p.21: Rod Williams/Bruce Coleman Collection; p.22: Kim Taylor/Bruce Coleman Collection; p.23: Satoshi Kuribayashi/Oxford Scientific Films; p.24: Scott Camuzine/Oxford Scientific Films; p.25: Tim Shepherd/Oxford Scientific Films; p.27: Aldo Brando/Oxford Scientific Films; p.28: J.A.L.Cooke/Oxford Scientific Films; p.29: Mike Birkhead/Oxford Scientific Films; p.30: Stephen J.Krasemann/Bruce Coleman Collection; p.31: J.A.L.Cooke/Oxford Scientific Films; p.32: Luiz Claudio Marigo/Bruce Coleman Collection; p.33: K.G.Preston-Mafham/Premaphotos; p.34: K.G.Preston-Mafham/Premaphotos; p.35: Anthony Bannister/Natural History Photographic Agency; p.36: Kim Taylor/Bruce Coleman Collection; p.38: Brian Hawkes/Natural History Photographic Agency; p.39: Dr. J.A.L.Cooke/Oxford Scientific Films; p.40: Christer Frederikson/Bruce Coleman Collection; p.41: Gunter Ziesler/Bruce Coleman Collection; p.42: Kim Taylor/Bruce Coleman Collection; p.43 top: Bruce Coleman Collection; p.43 bottom: K.G.Preston-Mafham/Premaphotos.

Index